Discovery KIDS™

Spin-the-Wheel
AWESOME
Oceans

LIVE. LEARN. DISCOVER.

PaRragon

Bath · New York · Singapore · Hong Kong · Cologne · Delhi · Melbourne

Bottlenose Dolphin

Dolphin Code Breaker

Dolphins talk to each other using a series of clicks and squeaks. Use the code breaker to crack the code, then write the answer in the space below to discover some interesting facts about the bottlenose dolphin.

a. The bottlenose dolphin is a small

_ _ _ _ _.

b. A baby bottlenose dolphin is called a

_ _ _ _.

c. The bottlenose dolphin's mouth is called a

_ _ _ _ _.

2

True or False

Bottlenose dolphins are related to orcas.

True ☐   False ☐

Wheel Quiz:

What does a bottlenose dolphin eat?

a. Fish and squid
b. Coral
c. Plankton

Blue Whale

Whale Math

Solve the problems to find out some interesting facts about the blue whale.

This giant animal eats tons of tiny shrimplike animals called krill. It sifts the krill through comblike teeth called baleen.

How much does a blue whale weigh?

$100 + 75 - 15 =$ ___

Answer: ___ tons

How far can a blue whale travel on its annual migration?

$8,000 + 4,500 - 7,500 =$ ___

Answer: ___ miles

How long is a newborn blue whale?

$12 + 16 - 3 =$ ___

Answer: ___ feet

Match the Shadow

Which of these shadows matches the blue whale?

Put a check in the yellow box by the correct shadow.

Wheel Quiz:

What is the endangered status of the blue whale?

a. High
b. Medium
c. Low

5

Shark Cross Out

Cross out the numbers in the table below, then copy the remaining letters into the boxes to discover a special fact about the great white shark.

4	6	T	5	E	6	7	E	8	9	T	3	4	H	5	7
3	T	5	3	6	R	I	7	8	A	8	N	G	2	L	E
5	6	8	S	4	5	E	3	R	2	R	A	T	E	7	D

The great white shark has 3,000 _ _ _ _ _ up to 2 inches long. Each one is shaped like a _ _ _ _ _ _ _ _ and has a _ _ _ _ _ _ _ _ edge like a steak knife.

Label the Picture

Write the correct numbers into the yellow circles to label this fierce shark.

1. Mouth
2. Nostril
3. Eye
4. Gills
5. Fin

DiscoveryFact™

A great white shark can smell a drop of blood in the water from up to 3 miles away.

Wheel Quiz:

How long is a great white shark?

a. Up to 6.5 feet
b. Up to 13 feet
c. Up to 20 feet

7

Great Barracuda

Word Search

There are five words hidden in the squares below. They are the names of the barracuda's favorite food. Can you find them all?

SARDINES
SILVERSIDE
MULLET
GOBY
HERRING

D E E S A R D I N E S
A L G J K A L Z B E I
M U L L E T D I A R L
T P P L E E E H T M V
H H M L Z C S B O I E
C A O G I Y B O G T R
A N I I Y R E J L E S
H T K M O M K E E E I
F R U I U B A A L K D
H E R R I N G H E R E
E G L H B L R E S A H

Fish Food

Which fish is which?
Match the names with
the correct fish.

Anchovies

Grouper

Jack fish

DiscoveryFact™

At a speed of
28 miles per hour,
the barracuda can
swim faster than
most prey for
short bursts.

Wheel Quiz:

Where does the
great barracuda live?

a. Worldwide
b. Atlantic Ocean
c. Pacific Ocean

Polar Bear

The polar bear cubs are trapped on the ice floe. Help the mother polar bear swim back to find them.

Polar Bear Maze

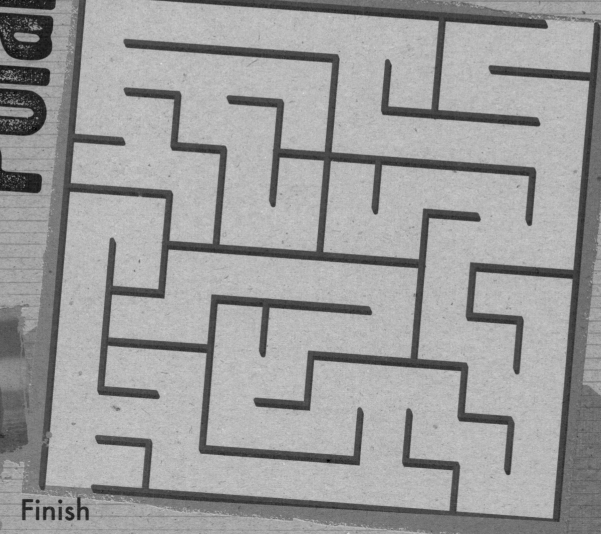

Start

Finish

Hidden Bear Food

Seals are the polar bear's favorite food. How many seal pups can you find on the page?

Polar bears have a coat of waterproof fur and a layer of fatty blubber 1.2 inches thick to keep them warm.

Wheel Quiz:

What do polar bears eat?

a. Grass
b. Krill
c. Fish, seals, seabirds

odd one out

walrus

Take a close look at the walruses below. One walrus in each row is different from the others. Put a check next to each one that is different.

a   b   c

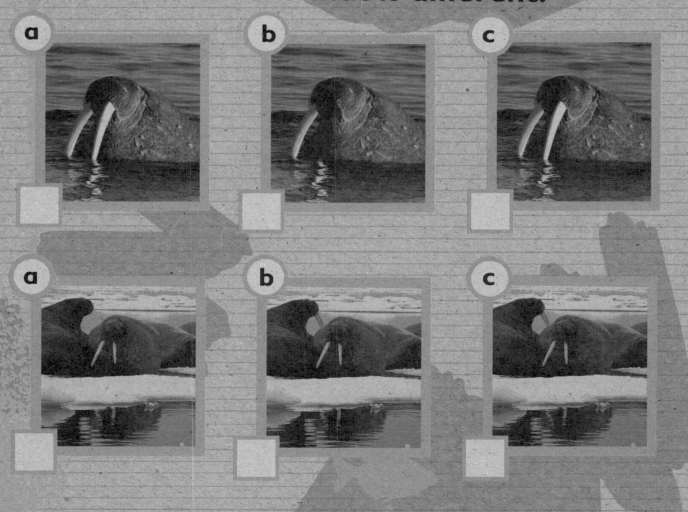

a   b   c

Walrus True or False

The walrus has an air sac in its throat to help it stay afloat.

True ☐   False ☐

DiscoveryFact™

The walrus has two tusks that grow up to 20 inches long. The tusks break the ice to make breathing holes.

Wheel Quiz:

How big is a walrus?

a. Up to 5 feet
b. Up to 8.5 feet
c. Up to 12 feet

Word Scramble

Unscramble the letters in each word below to discover an interesting fact about the gray seal.

orfyt   htriyt

The female gray seal can live up to _ _ _ _ _ years in the wild and male gray seals up to _ _ _ _ _ _ _ years.

What Does It Mean?

Seals belong to a group of animals called pinnipeds. Can you guess what *pinniped* means? Circle the correct answer.

Clue: Look carefully at the back flippers.

a. *Pinniped* means "winged foot."
b. *Pinniped* means "water tail."
c. *Pinniped* means "fairy fins."

Wheel Quiz:

What is the gray seal's endangered status?

a. High
b. Medium
c. Low

Gentoo Penguin

Penguins have to swim fast to escape from predators. The names of three predators are hidden in the squares below. Can you find them all?

Penguin Word Search

N	A	D	L	A	D	S	E	T	T	Y
E	G	H	E	Y	D	A	L	J	O	O
L	E	C	O	E	L	A	S	R	I	R
L	M	A	P	E	I	T	T	A	C	C
A	Y	R	A	Y	O	R	T	C	Y	A
R	N	R	R	A	N	E	E	U	D	W
I	A	D	D	K	S	B	L	L	A	H
S	L	C	S	J	C	L	R	L	L	E
G	E	I	E	I	O	U	O	E	B	L
E	M	N	A	M	T	H	C	N	H	E
N	O	I	L	A	E	S	Y	D	S	A

Sea lion
Leopard seal
Orca

16

Neat Nest

Unscramble the letters to finish the sentences about gentoo penguins and their nests.

The gentoo penguin makes a circular T E N S from P B B E S L E , grass, or sticks.

Then it S Y L A two S G E G that C A T H H five weeks later.

At about H E R E T months old, the S H I K C C grow their T U D L A feathers.

Wheel Quiz:

What do gentoo penguins eat?

a. Crustaceans, fish, squid
b. Leaves
c. Seaweed

Word Maze

Ancient mariners told tales of a sea monster called the kraken, which may have been a giant squid. Find your way across the maze below by coloring the boxes to spell the words: *sea monster.*

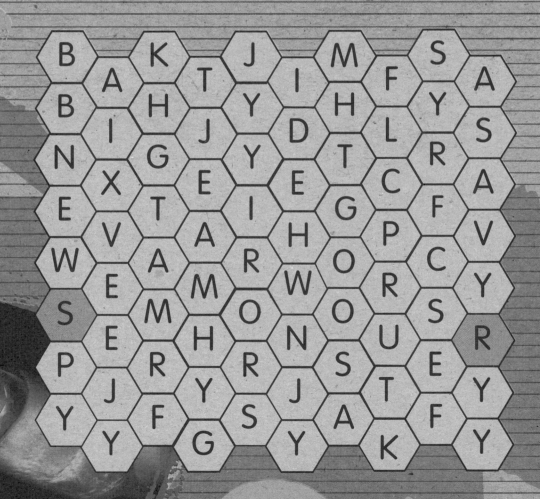

Sea Monster

Draw your own sea monster based on the giant squid.

The giant squid has the largest eyes in the animal kingdom, measuring some 10 inches across.

Wheel Quiz:

Where can you find the giant squid?

a. Worldwide
b. Arctic and Antarctic oceans
c. Nowhere—they are extinct

Moray Eel

Follow the Trail

This damselfish will make a tasty snack for the moray eel.

Follow the trails to find out which one ends up in the eel's hidden lair.

a

b

c

DiscoveryFact™

The moray eel has a second set of jaws. Once prey is caught, the second set of jaws drags the food down its throat.

Spot the Difference

Can you find five differences between these two pictures?

QUIZ

How much do you know about ocean animals? Try this quiz, then use your wheel to check your answers.

1. Which is largest?
   a. Blue whale
   b. Polar bear
   c. Giant squid

2. What is from the Antarctic?
   a. Walrus
   b. Great white shark
   c. Gentoo penguin

3. Which animal is endangered?
   a. Gentoo penguin
   b. Gray seal
   c. Blue whale

4. Which animal eats plankton?
   a. Green turtle
   b. Sea urchin
   c. Moon jellyfish

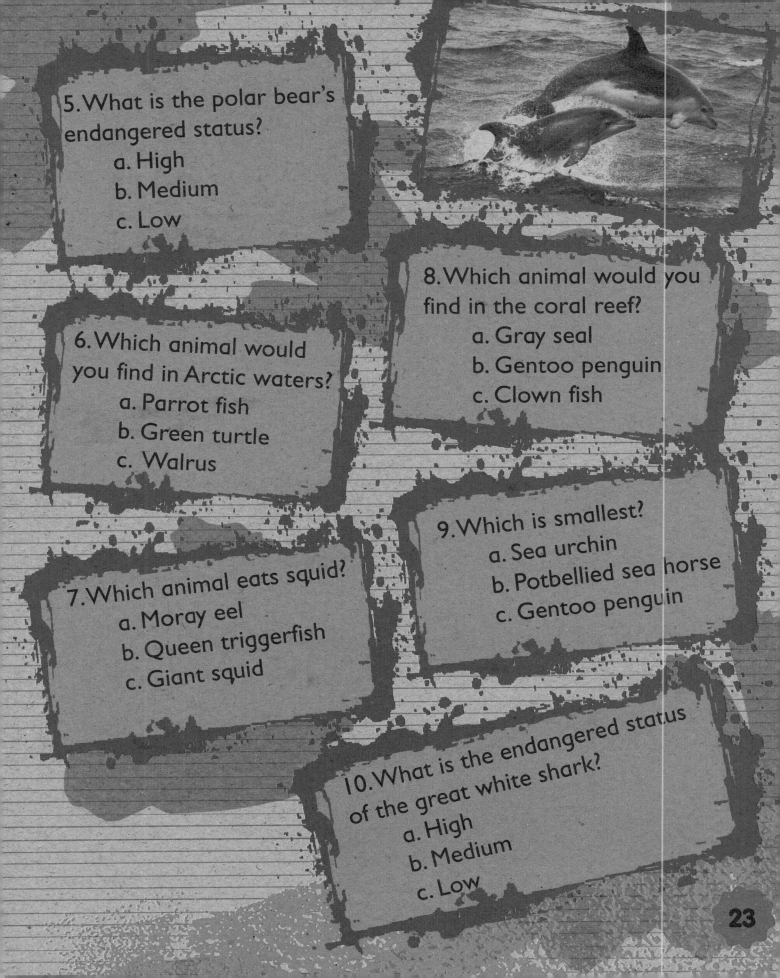

5. What is the polar bear's endangered status?
   a. High
   b. Medium
   c. Low

6. Which animal would you find in Arctic waters?
   a. Parrot fish
   b. Green turtle
   c. Walrus

7. Which animal eats squid?
   a. Moray eel
   b. Queen triggerfish
   c. Giant squid

8. Which animal would you find in the coral reef?
   a. Gray seal
   b. Gentoo penguin
   c. Clown fish

9. Which is smallest?
   a. Sea urchin
   b. Potbellied sea horse
   c. Gentoo penguin

10. What is the endangered status of the great white shark?
   a. High
   b. Medium
   c. Low

Orca

Orca Shapes

Look at the picture above. Then circle the shadow that matches the picture exactly.

Whale True or False?

Orca live and hunt on their own.

True ☐ False ☐

DiscoveryFact™

Mother orca give birth every three to ten years, after a 17-month pregnancy.

Wheel Quiz:

What food does an orca eat?

a. Plankton
b. Seaweed
c. Fish, sharks, and marine animals

Moon Jellyfish

Spot the Difference

Can you find five differences between the two pictures below?

Jelly Shadows

Look at the photo, then circle the shadow that matches the picture exactly.

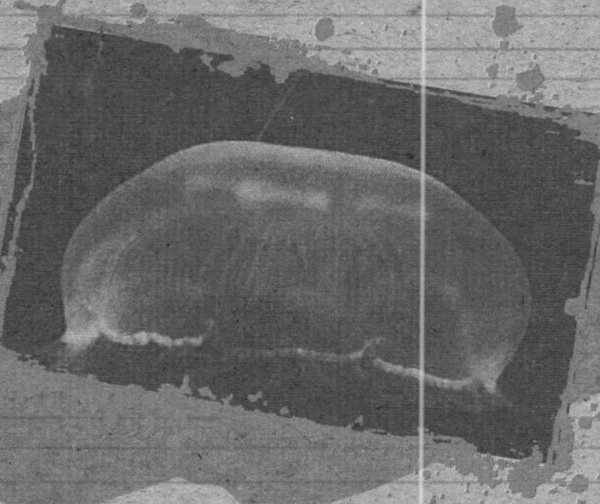

DiscoveryFact™

The moon jellyfish gathers its food by dragging its long tentacles through the water and entangling tiny sea creatures.

Wheel Quiz:

What is the moon jellyfish's endangered status?

a. High
b. Medium
c. Low

Take a look at the close-up pictures of parts of a turtle below. Match the labels with the right picture.

CloSe-uP

1. Flipper
2. Tail

3. Shell
4. Beak

Turtle Doodle

Draw a turtle in the space below.

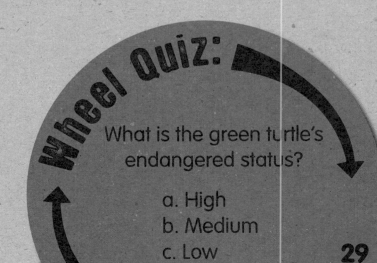

Wheel Quiz:

What is the green turtle's endangered status?

a. High
b. Medium
c. Low

Hammerhead Shark

Shark Tangle

a   b   c

This hammerhead shark can smell some prey, but it doesn't know which way to go across the ocean floor. See if you can help it out!

The correct line is ____.

Spot the Difference

Can you find four differences between these two pictures?

Can you find five differences between these two pictures?

Hammerheads have special sensors in their heads that detect electricity given off by living beings. This helps them find prey.

Wheel Quiz:

How big can a hammerhead shark grow?

a. Up to 12 feet
b. Up to 20 feet
c. Up to 5 feet

Sea Urchin Word Search

M	C	R	I	N	O	I	D
U	B	E	E	S	S	U	M
S	R	A	S	P	P	J	N
S	I	L	I	P	O	L	A
E	T	G	D	C	N	K	K
L	T	A	E	W	G	Z	E
H	L	E	R	I	E	K	S
A	E	S	T	A	R	U	Q

The five words hidden in the squares above are the names of the sea urchin's favorite foods. Can you find them all?

Algae
Mussel
Sponge
Brittle star
Crinoid

Urchin

Urchin Calculator Code

Crack the number code to finish the sentence.

1	2	3	4	5	6	7	8	9	10
C	D	E	H	I	M	N	O	R	S

The sea urchin belongs to a group of animals with spiky outer skins called

3 1 4 5 7 8 2 3 9 6 10

_ _ _ _ _ _ _ _ _ _ _

DiscoveryFact™

The sea urchin moves along the ocean floor using tiny, tube-shaped feet and stiff, spiky spines that can move in its shell.

Wheel Quiz:

How big does a sea urchin grow?

a. Up to 31 inches
b. Up to 3 inches
c. Up to 7 inches

Shadows

Look at the picture above. Then circle the shadow that matches the picture exactly.

DiscoveryFact™

The male sea horse carries the female's eggs in his pouch until they are ready to hatch.

Label the Picture

Fill in the correct numbers to label this male sea horse.

1. Mouth
2. Snout
3. Eye
4. Dorsal Fin
5. Pouch
6. Tail

Wheel Quiz:

What does a potbellied sea horse eat?

a. Mammals
b. Fish
c. Crustaceans

Parrot Fish

Cross Out

Cross out the numbers in the table below, then copy the remaining letters into the boxes to discover a special fact about the parrot fish.

4	6	M	5	A	6	7	L	8	9	E	3	4	F	5	7
3	E	5	7	6	M	A	L	8	E	8	C	O	2	L	O
5	2	R	S	4	5	D	3	I	2	E	S	5	M	7	A
L	5	7	1	E	3	6	C	H	5	4	A	7	N	G	É

_ _ _ _ and _ _ _ _ _ _ parrot fish are different _ _ _ _ _ _.
If a male parrot fish _ _ _ _, a female will turn into a
_ _ _ _ and _ _ _ _ _ _ color.

Color Fish

Design your own parrot fish in the space below.

The parrot fish gets its name because the teeth on its top and bottom jaws are joined together. They look like a parrot's beak.

Wheel Quiz:

How big is a parrot fish?

a. 1.2–1.6 inches
b. 5–5.5 inches
c. 12–15.7 inches

Triggerfish
Word Scramble

Unscramble the letters in the word below to discover an interesting fact about the clown triggerfish.

Humu-humu-nuku-nuku-apuaa or Humu humu for short, are the nicknames of the triggerfish in: W A I H A I

_ _ _ _ _ _

Spot the Difference

Can you spot four differences between these two queen triggerfish?

The triggerfish has a long spine in its top fin. When it needs to hide, it can lock the spine and wedge itself in small spaces.

Wheel Quiz:

What is the queen triggerfish's endangered status?

a. High
b. Medium
c. Low

White-Spotted Puffer Fish

Puffer Fish Trail

Follow the trail to find out which of these sea creatures is the puffer fish's predator.

a.

b.

c.

Word Search

Can you find these words in the squares below? They are all names of different kinds of puffer fish.

B	T	S	B	F	Y	X	Y	J	K	H
A	O	C	W	I	C	K	E	H	X	S
L	A	U	K	E	W	D	S	Y	H	I
L	D	I	H	S	L	I	A	I	I	F
O	F	O	U	T	F	L	F	A	G	W
O	I	L	J	L	T	L	F	C	N	O
N	S	O	L	N	C	Y	B	I	U	L
F	H	E	V	E	O	C	M	E	S	B
I	W	K	N	L	G	J	A	P	G	H
S	H	S	I	F	E	B	O	L	G	B
H	B	U	B	B	L	E	F	I	S	H

BALLOON FISH
BLOWFISH
BUBBLE FISH
GLOBEFISH
SWELLFISH
TOADFISH

DiscoveryFact™

When the puffer fish is threatened, it puffs itself up to twice its size to avoid being eaten.

Wheel Quiz:

How big is the puffer fish?

a. Up to 4 inches
b. Up to 10 inches
c. Up to 3 feet

Clown Fish

Odd One Out

Take a close look at the clown fish below.

One fish in each row is different. Check the box next to the different fish.

a

b

c

a

b

c

Count the all Clown Fish

How many clown fish can you count on these pages?

The clown fish lives among the poisonous sea anemone. The fish is covered with a slimy coating that stops it from being stung.

Wheel Quiz:

What does a clown fish eat?

a. Corals, sponges
b. Sea urchins
c. Algae, mollusks, crustaceans

Ocean Animals

Word Search

Can you find these words hidden in the squares below? They are all types of food eaten by ocean animals.

ALGAE
EEL
CRAB
FISH
PLANKTON
SEA URCHIN
SEAL
SHELLFISH
SHRIMP
SQUID

A	Q	O	B	F	Y	X	Y	J	N	P
L	F	C	R	A	B	K	E	T	I	L
G	S	U	K	N	W	D	X	Y	H	A
A	I	I	H	S	I	F	A	R	C	N
E	E	L	U	T	R	N	O	A	R	K
R	Z	L	J	U	T	K	O	C	U	T
A	S	H	R	I	M	P	B	C	A	O
T	S	L	V	M	O	C	M	E	E	N
S	H	E	L	L	F	I	S	H	S	E
E	R	K	N	O	O	K	N	R	L	P
S	Q	U	I	D	P	K	L	A	E	S

Ocean Food

Eel

Can you match the food with the animals that eat it?

Fish

Moray eel

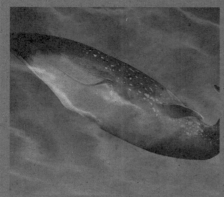

Blue whale

Algae

Polar bear

Plankton

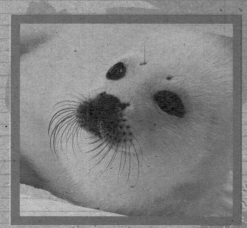

Seal

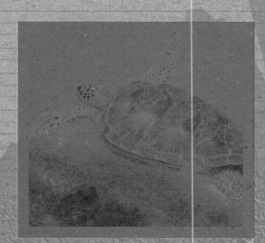

Green turtle

Gray seal

45

ANSWERS

Page 2
Dolphin Code Breaker
a. Whale
b. Calf
c. Beak

Page 3
Dolphin True or False
True, they are related to orcas.

Wheel Quiz
a. Fish and squid

Page 4
Whale Math
160 tons; 5,000 miles; 25 feet

Page 5
Match the Shadow

Wheel Quiz
a. High

Page 6
Shark Cross Out
teeth; triangle; serrated

Page 7
Label the Picture

Wheel Quiz
c. Up to 20 feet

Page 8
Word Search

Page 9
Fish Food

Anchovies

Jack fish

Grouper

Wheel Quiz
a. Worldwide

Page 10
Polar Bear Maze

Page 11
Hidden Bear Food
There are 16 seals

Wheel Quiz
c. Fish, seals, seabirds

Page 12
Walrus Odd One Out

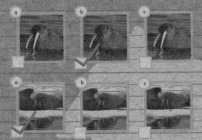

Page 13
True or False
True, the air sac acts like a buoy helping the walrus to keep its head above the water.

Wheel Quiz
c. Up to 12 feet

Page 14
Word Scramble
forty; thirty

Page 15
What Does It Mean?
a. winged foot

Wheel Quiz
c. Low

Page 16
Penguin Word Search

Page 17
Neat Nest
NEST; PEBBLES; LAYS; EGGS; HATCH; THREE; CHICKS; ADULT

Wheel Quiz
a. Crustaceans, fish, squid

Page 18
Word Maze

Wheel Quiz
a. Worldwide

Page 20
Follow the Trail
Trail b

Page 21
Spot the difference

Wheel Quiz
c. Up to 13 feet

Page 22-23
1.a; 2.c; 3.c; 4.c; 5.a;
6.c; 7.c; 8.c; 9.a; 10.b

Page 24
Odd One Out

Page 25
True or False
False, orcas hunt in pods

Wheel Quiz
c. Fish, sharks, and marine animals

Page 26
Spot the Difference

Page 27
Jelly Shadows

Wheel Quiz
c. Low

Page 28
Green Turtle Close-up

Page 29
Wheel Quiz
a. High

Page 30
Shark Tangle
Line b

Page 31
Spot the Difference

Wheel Quiz
b. Up to 20 feet

Page 32
Word Search

M	C	R	I	N	O	I	D
U	B	E	E	S	S	U	M
S	R	A	S	P	P	J	N
S	I	L	I	P	O	L	A
E	T	G	D	C	N	K	K
L	T	A	E	W	G	Z	E
H	L	E	R	I	E	K	S
A	E	S	T	A	R	U	Q

Page 33
Urchin Calculator Code:
ECHINODERMS

Wheel Quiz
c. Up to 7 inches

Page 34
Shadows

Page 35
Label the Picture

Wheel Quiz
c. Crustaceans

Page 36
Cross Out
MALE; FEMALE; COLORS;
DIES; MALE; CHANGE

Page 37
Wheel Quiz
c. 12-15.7 inches

Page 38
Word Scramble
HAWAII

Page 39
Spot the difference

Wheel Quiz
b. Medium

Page 40
Trail a.

Page 41
Word Search

A	T	S	B	F	Y	X	Y	J	K	H
A	O	C	W	I	C	K	E	H	X	S
L	A	U	K	E	W	D	S	Y	H	I
L	D	I	H	S	L	I	A	I	I	F
O	F	O	U	T	F	L	F	A	G	W
O	I	L	J	L	T	L	F	C	N	O
N	S	O	L	N	C	Y	B	I	U	L
F	H	E	V	E	O	C	M	E	S	B
I	W	K	N	L	G	J	A	P	G	H
S	H	S	I	F	E	B	O	L	G	B
H	B	U	B	B	L	E	F	I	S	H

Wheel Quiz
c. Up to 3 feet

Page 42
Row 1, b is the odd one out
Row 2, a is the odd one out

Page 43
Count the Clown Fish
There are 22 in total

Wheel Quiz
c. Algae, mollusks, crustaceans

Page 44
Word Search

A	Q	O	B	F	Y	X	Y	J	N	P
L	F	C	R	A	B	K	E	T	I	L
G	S	U	K	N	W	D	X	Y	H	A
A	I	H	S	I	P	A	R	C	N	
E	E	D	U	T	R	N	O	A	R	K
R	Z	L	J	U	T	K	O	C	U	T
A	S	H	R	I	M	P	B	C	A	O
T	S	L	V	M	O	C	M	E	E	N
S	H	E	L	L	F	I	S	H	S	E
E	R	K	N	O	O	K	N	A	L	P
S	Q	U	I	D	P	K	L	A	E	S

Page 45
Algae = green turtle
Eel = gray seal
Fish = moray eel
Plankton = blue whale
Seal = polar bear

Credits/ Acknowledgments

b = bottom, t = top, r = right, l = left, c = center

Front cover b Getty/Gail Shumway c istockphoto/Serdar Yagci, istockphoto/Grzegorz Choi_ski, r Getty/Sergio Pitamitz. Inside front cover t istockphoto/Chris Dascher, b Getty/Daisy Gilardini.

Back cover istockphoto/Oliver Anlauf

Wheel front clockwise from dolphin: istockphoto/George Clerk, Getty/Purestock, istockphoto/Bart Coenders, istockphoto/Dennis Sabo, istockphoto/John Pitcher, istockphoto/Pauline Mills, istockphoto/Sean Morris, istockphoto, Getty/Brian J. Skerry, istockphoto/Bryan Faust. Wheel reverse clockwise from sea horse: istockphoto, istockphoto/ Richard Carey, istockphoto/Ian Scott, istockphoto/Jodi Jacobson, istockphoto/Luís Fernando Curci Chavier, istockphoto/ Evgeniya Lazareva, istockphoto/Klaas Lingbeek-van Kranen, 28 istockphoto/Christophe Péricé, stockphoto/Ian Scott, istockphoto/Derek Holzapfel. 1 istockphoto/Kristian Sekulic, 2bl istockphoto/Francisco Romero, 2br istockphoto/George Clerk, 3c istockphoto/Kristian Sekulic, 3b istockphoto/Jose Manuel Gelpi Diaz, 4 Getty/Purestock, 7 istockphoto/Keith Flood, 8 istockphoto/Richard Brooks, 9bl istockphoto/Klaas Lingbeek, 10t istockphoto/Erlend Kvalsvik, 10b istockphoto/ John Pitcher, 11tr istockphoto/David T. Gomez, 11 istockphoto/Vladimir Melnik, 12t istockphoto/Gail A Johnson, 12b istockphoto/Pauline Mills, 13t istockphoto/Pauline Mills, 13b istockphoto/Gail A Johnson, 14 Getty/Frank Greenaway, 15t Getty/Tom Brakefield, 15b Getty/Frank Greenaway, 16t Getty/Daisy Gilardini, 16b Getty/Sergio Pitamitz, 18 Getty/ Brian J. Skerry, 20t istockphoto/Bryan Faust, 20b istockphoto/Nancy Nehring, 21 istockphoto, 22t Getty/Sergio Pitamitz, 22b Getty/Frank Greenaway, 23 istockphoto/George Clerk, 24 istockphoto/Evgeniya Lazareva, 25t istockphoto/ Jami Garrison, 25b istockphoto/Evgeniya Lazareva, 25br istockphoto/Jon Helgason, 26 istockphoto/Klaas Lingbeek-van Kranen, 28 istockphoto/Christophe Péricé, 29 istockphoto/Christophe Péricé, 30t istockphoto/Ian Scott, 30b istockphoto/Mark Kostich, 33 istockphoto/Derek Holzapfel, 34 istockphoto, 35 istockphoto, 36 istockphoto/Richard Carey, 38tr Dreamstime/Conchasdiver, 38b istockphoto/Ian Scott, 40t istockphoto/Jodi Jacobson, 40bl istockphoto/ Cor Bosman, 40bc istockphoto/Derek Holzapfel, 40br istockphoto/George Clerk, 42t istockphoto/Luís Fernando Curci Chavier, 42b istockphoto/Michal Galazka, 44 istockphoto/Richard Carey.

Font: Hotel Coral Essex by Pennyzine / Jason Ramirez.

Written by Cathy Jones
Consultant Gerald Legg

First published by Parragon in 2010

Parragon
Queen Street House
4 Queen Street
Bath BA1 1HE, UK

ISBN 978-1-4075-9271-8

Printed in Malaysia